Brides
in
VOGUE

Brides
in
VOGUE

SINCE 1910

Christina Probert

THAMES AND HUDSON

ACKNOWLEDGMENTS

Vogue has always covered society weddings and brides' fashion in detail. Recently, the latter has become an increasingly important fashion area, and Condé Nast now produces specialized magazines on the subject. Three of them – *Brides, Vogue Jeune Mariée* and *Vogue Sposa* – are the sources of some of the later pictures reproduced here, and I am indebted to their editors and contributors, as well as to those of *Vogue*, for this material. I would like to thank Alex Kroll for his guidance throughout, Bunny Cantor, Patrick Handley and Timothy Hyde for their help with research, Liz Prior and Elizabeth Wickham for the book's design, and Charlie Lee-Potter for her major contribution to the book in terms of research, planning, advice and last-minute captioning.

C.P.

To
Edmund and Belinda
Angie and Chris
Rea and Simon

Text filmset in Great Britain by Tameside Filmsetting Limited
Printed and bound in Japan
by Dai Nippon

Cover. IV 1983 Francois Lamy. *Jean-Louis Scherrer.* Back cover. BV 1920.
Page 2. FV 1982 Guy Bourdin. *Hubert de Givenchy.*

CONTENTS

Key to captions

Information is given in the following order: edition; artist or photographer;
designer or maker (the last always in *italic*). Editions are identified by initials:

AV American *Vogue*
BV British *Vogue*
FV French *Vogue*
IV Italian *Vogue*

INTRODUCTION

'A woman seldom asks advice before she has bought her wedding clothes.'
Joseph Addison (1672–1719)

The lodestar of any wedding day is surely that long-dreamt-about dress, for centuries considered an auspicious garment. For the Romans it was yellow, considered the most propitious colour, worn with matching shoes and the yellow veil which was sacred to Hymen, the god of marriage. Subsequently, the veil went out of fashion until the classical revival in dress in the late eighteenth century. In the Middle Ages and on into the Renaissance the bride's dress was a vehicle for the display of her family's wealth and influence in its use of gold and silver threads, imported and perhaps specially woven fabrics, and lavish jewelling. Colour, too, was often decided by family colours and crests, and the style followed that of general fashion. By the late eighteenth century the new status symbol was the white wedding dress; it gave the impression that the bride was a lady of leisure, and her family wealthy enough to provide a dress which would only be worn once. In fact, for the less wealthy, the dress was often made with a separate bodice and skirt, so that the latter could be adapted for later wear. Among the wealthier, the dress very often became a balldress for a season.

Many of the wedding customs which we regard as traditional and long established originated only in the nineteenth century. Although white had been popular for weddings in earlier periods, it was not until the nineteenth century that its symbolism of purity acquired prime importance and it became firmly established as the most popular wedding colour right up to the present day. The idea that any bride who does not wear white is not a virgin is a purely modern affectation: most nineteenth- and early twentieth-century silk dresses were creamy white, and in fact silver tissue and pastel colours were smart choices during the early twentieth century. The Victorians imbued not only fabric colours, but more importantly the types of flower in the bouquet, with deep significance. Red roses, as we all know, signify passionate love; orange blossom, the most popular bride's flower during the first two decades of this century, meant 'Your purity equals your loveliness.' The origins of the lucky shoe lie in its significance as an emblem of possession, illustrated by the tale of Cinderella and the glass slipper which the prince used to claim her, and in its fertility symbolism; thus the bride, when she used to throw her shoe into the crowd of guests, was throwing

Helen Lee Worthing, renowned theatrical beauty, in a Marie Antoinette wedding ensemble designed by De Meyer. Fantastical and retrospective, the gown reflects the contemporary vogue for extensive veiling and extravagant trimming.
A V 1920 De Meyer. *De Meyer*

1910

Heavy lace, drapery and huge beribboned bouquets. AV 1913 Walter Keyser Bachrach

Pared-down silhouette with quintessential overdress, embroidered and beaded. AV 1918 De Meyer. *Callot*

some of her own good luck at some unsuspecting unmarried friend. The bouquet has now taken over this role, the shoe now being tied to the going-away vehicle, used in miniature on the wedding cake, or even in the bouquet, for luck.

Between 1910 and 1920 the wedding ensemble changed dramatically. Common practice at the outset of the decade decreed a long, lightly draped dress with natural or high waistline, often with a crossover bodice. Sleeves were long and tight, to compensate for the long gloves once worn by the bride and now moving out of fashion. A long and often heavily ornamented court train – with bows, embroidery, brocading and/or beading – completed the ensemble. Headdresses and veils varied, but hair was always put up and back, well away from the neck to give maximum emphasis to the ubiquitous string of pearls. Very often a circlet of orange blossom (a flower to be found somewhere on almost every bridal ensemble) or pearls held the veil, which covered the whole head, rarely the face. Old family veils were the most popular, in heavy Brussels lace or the lighter rose-point variety, but fine tulle edged with lace or embroidery was also coming into fashion. Much emphasis was laid on the bouquet, which might measure as much as two feet across, and was a lavish confection of flowers, greenery and trailing ribbons with individual flower heads knotted into them.

By 1913 the dress was shorter, revealing the inevitable white satin slippers, ornamented, now that they were on display, with rosettes, jewels or flowers. *Vogue* noted in 1914 that 'there is no denying that the short skirt and short veil make the average bride look at least three years younger than she is', and indeed shorter dresses stayed in fashion. The long court train was still part of the wedding ensemble, but it was now quite narrow and much less heavily ornamented. The veil was also becoming lighter and lighter, and lace lost popularity in favour of the finer hemmed tulle or chiffon.

The wedding dresses of the last three years of the decade were characterized by their rather informal lean lines – the waist level no longer being very important – and by their exquisite detailing and ornamentation. As lingerie layers beneath the dress decreased, delicate overdresses became popular. 'Will it never return,' said *Vogue* in 1917, 'that chaste garment, severely plain, with its stark, gleaming train?' Full rein was given not only to the skills of the couturier, but to those of the embroideress and the lacemaker, who produced ethereal draperies embroidered with pearls, white jet or crystals, Art Nouveau-embroidered satin dresses, silver lace and embroidered silver tissue.

The dress itself was shorter and lighter in both weight and appearance by 1916. The melon silhouette (narrow-shouldered, draped widely over the torso and hips, shaped into a narrow, calf-level hemline) and the full-skirted shepherdess look formed some of the smartest wedding dresses in 1916 and

1917. 'Medieval' dresses and headdresses were very popular, too, in mid-decade, incorporating features such as huge flowing sleeves, high waistlines or low hip-belts emphasized with beaded braid, and nun-like veils which covered head and neck, leaving only the face itself peeping out. Another favourite style was that modelled on one's mother's or grandmother's wedding attire, using antique lace and family jewels. 'In the matter of the veil and the coiffure', said *Vogue* in 1918, 'individual fancy runs riot'. Veils were indeed varied, in lace, tulle or silver tissue, sometimes embroidered, headdresses too, but hairstyles were still the traditional up-and-back shape. Bouquets were now smaller, simpler. Most popular flowers were lilies of the valley, orange blossom, orchids and gardenias with ferns. The supremacy of satin was now challenged by brocade, panné velvet, voile, tulle and lace.

The most popular wedding of the decade was that of Princess Patricia of Connaught to Commander Alexander Robert Maule Ramsay RN in 1919. It was a true love match; 'even a princess may prefer romance to royalty', noted *Vogue*, as Princess Patricia became simply Lady Victoria Ramsay in order to move closer to her husband in rank. Her wedding dress was an exquisite creation of brocaded cream panné velvet with a train of silver cloth embroidered in lilies with raised stamens, her veil a lace heirloom.

Young married friends were considered the most suitable bridesmaids in 1909, but by 1914 the modern custom of asking unmarried friends to be bridesmaids had become established. Their dresses were designed to echo that of the bride, most often in white or cream, with contrasting sash, worn with caps or picture hats. Later styles echoed the fashion for fine overtunics; coloured satin was used beneath creamy tulle to create soft pastel colours. The bouffant skirts which were smart mid-decade were particularly so for bridesmaids, sometimes caught up at the front or sides to reveal contrast-coloured underskirts. Unlike the bride, the bridesmaids were permitted to have their hair down, loosely pinned up or plaited; their flowers were smaller versions of the bride's bouquet.

The stress of preparing for a large wedding was much the same in 1913 as it is now, it seems: 'there should be a propaganda . . . against the nerve-racking preparation for a fashionable wedding', said *Vogue*. A new custom was to hold weddings in the privacy of a country house, but the number of guests, lengthy preparations and entertainment were just as lavish. Not even the Great War had much effect on the smart wedding – except for the uncertainty until the last minute as to the bridegroom's presence. Dorothy Parker remarked in *Vogue*: 'It takes two to play a War Wedding March – one plays "here comes the bride" the other "there goes the groom"'! The latter, in his smart uniform, began to play a more colourful role in the event, and the bride could console herself with the fact that, as *Vogue* noted, her dress looked 'all the fairer beside a soldier husband's uniform'.

Princess Patricia's very formal wedding dress, heavy with symbolism and antique lace. BV 1919 *Reville and Rossiter*

Youthful flower girl in huge leghorn hat, organdie frock. BV 1918

1920

BV 1919 De Meyer. *Joseph*

AV 1911 Aimé Dupont

AV 1918 *Idare*

Bridesmaids of the decade ranged from demure to sophisticated. Directoire-style bridesmaids, *above*, in satin-lined poke bonnets, carrying old-fashioned posies. *Right*, the bergère look, a full grey satin frock embroidered with pink and green sprigs and, *below*, four eligible young ladies in calf-length champagne-coloured lace and satin girdled with sage green. The bridal cortège's headgear,

above, echoes the huge-crowned hats in fashion generally, and their bouquets are sized to match. The bridesmaids, *below*, wear long, buttoned gloves which, once essential, had now become a matter of choice. Veiled dresses were as popular for bridesmaids as for brides, such as the flesh-coloured frock *opposite*, veiled with cream lace and cafe-au-lait chiffon.

AV 1914 Rochlitz Studio

AV 1913 Aimé Dupont

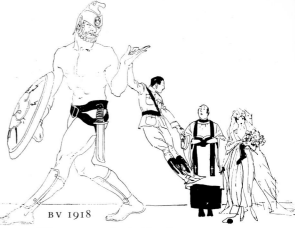

'Here comes the bride, there goes the
groom'; wartime weddings lost
nothing in grandeur, and gained in
glamour. Lanvin's daughter, Marguerite,
left, married René Jacquemaire in
Art-Deco-style jewel-embroidered
satin; Marie-Madeleine Allard, *below*,
married the Baron de Surville in
Turkish-draped silk voile.

AV 1914 Underwood & Underwood   AV 1918

Dorothy Harvey married Lieutenant Marcellus Thompson under a flowered pergola, *above left*; uniforms were so smart that Sylvanus Stokes, Jr., wore his Naval Reserve uniform for his marriage to Margaret Fahnestock, *above right*. Leta Sullivan married Lieutenant Albert Hoffman, *below*, with 11 bridesmaids in the new calf-length gowns.

AV 1918 Bachrach

13

The medieval look, *below*: huge sleeves, elongated bodice and swathed skirt. Bands embroidered with seed pearls, crystals and silver thread adorn neck and sleeves, and long silver tassels follow the lines of the panelled train.

BV 1918

The melon silhouette at its slimmest, *opposite*: the bridesmaid on the left wears a beige lace dress and a Niniche hat, the one on the right jade green chiffon, pastel silk flowers and a leghorn hat. The bride, centre, wears a charmeuse and Duchess lace dress with tassels, and headdress of pearls. Her lace veil is lined with pink chiffon.

One of the new breed of diaphanous headdresses, *above*, fashioned from strings of pearls and swathes of tulle.

BV 1919 Helen Dryden.
Helen Dryden

Donna Vivina Lanzo de Mazzarino's wedding dress, *right*, by Worth. Embroidered all over in white jet, silver and crystal, its tight sleeves and narrow train were fashion points, as was the lily attached to the left shoulder, matching the informal 'bouquet'.

BV 1919 *Worth*

1920

'Fashion has supplanted custom and individuality has supplanted both', wrote *Vogue* of contemporary wedding styles in 1923. Fashion, did, however, play a very important role in determining what would be worn at society weddings: the bridal hemline and outline followed general fashion assiduously. Certain conventions were still respected: 'no matter what hour the wedding is held, there must be no exaggerated décolletage, for Vogue considers the wedding in its traditional light as a religious ceremony.' And in France, long sleeves, gloves, and the court train remained traditional far longer than in Britain or America. Couturier wedding dresses, rather than designs made up by favourite dressmakers, became more prevalent as superficial ornamentation gave way to cut as the most important design factor in fashionable nuptials at the end of the decade.

At the outset of the twenties the medieval, or 'moyen âge', look was still very popular, and the low waist which accompanied it was a leitmotif of wedding dresses for most of the decade, accentuated by girdles, silver cords with long tassels, or flower garlands. A formal court train was still *de rigueur* and the most usual neckline square, its lower edge formed by a satin slip; shoulders and sleeves were in flimsy tulle, net or chiffon. The essential pearls had now become a waist-length single string. The silhouette was slender-torsoed, with a loosely draped or gathered skirt; fullness was light and bouffant, in tulle frills or filmy, satin-edged overdresses. Hemlines rose and rose, reaching knee-level mid-decade (the most daring level reached by wedding dresses, although skirts generally were shorter). The new cropped, shingled hairstyles were emphasized by headdresses which came low around the head, but were very fine and light – such as the popular bandeau and diadem shapes – and by transparent veiling or fine lace. Antique and family laces were still traditional choices, quite frequently in association with tulle; lace was used for gowns too, lined with rose, lemon or white satin. Satin was still the most popular fabric, but crepe de chine, taffeta, silver cloth, lamé and tissue now became important. Layers of tulle or chiffon formed overdresses, and velvet, white fox and ermine were winter choices.

For the first few years after the Great War, smart weddings in France were very restrained – indeed, some members of every large family seemed to be in mourning – and were usually held in the country. *Vogue* commented on suitable clothes for the second marriage of war widows – 'all that tends to display must be avoided' – and suggested that the mood should be 'serious and discreetly gay'. Lamé was not recommended: one elegant second bride wore mauve crepe de chine beaded with crystal and silver, a mauve tulle overdress, and hyacinths in her hair.

Two royal wedding dresses mixed tradition with fashion. Princess Mary, in 1922, wore a family Honiton lace veil and heavy, traditional court train embroidered with emblematic flowers. Her dress, however, was of silver

War widow's second wedding outfit, 'in excellent taste': beige satin with darker hat and gold tulle veil. B V 1920

lamé, the marquisette overdress embroidered with a trelliswork of pearls and beads. Lady Elizabeth Bowes-Lyon, in 1923, wore a veil edged with rare old lace lent her by the Queen. The dress itself was medieval Italian in influence, of ivory chiffon moiré with silver lamé bands ornamented with seed pearls. She wore both waist and shoulder trains. In 1921, the Duchess of Marlborough, her wedding being less formal, had worn gold lace especially woven in Burano to a design suggested by the Duke.

Wedding dresses shortened very gradually: first, drapery was used to give an uneven hemline, then layering, then a caught-up hipline or whole side to the dress. By 1926 the silhouette was straight, narrow and knee-length. The veil had shortened, too, but the court train was still some three yards long and had become ceremonial, rather than fashionable, dress. Now the most popular types *Vogue* noted were 'transparent from the shoulders down to the part below the waist . . . most subtle little curtained windows through which the audience can glimpse the figure of the bride as she advances up the aisle.' Some brides now wore sleeveless dresses, or very short sleeves, headdresses left much shingled hair exposed, the veil being fastened at the back, and the rather casual 'boat' neckline became very fashionable. The 'tendency of late years, slow in development, . . . to lessen the formality of the wedding gown', which *Vogue* had noted in 1923, reached its peak in 1926.

Superficial embellishment such as beading, lace and embroidery now began to disappear as superb cut became the focal point of the wedding dress. The slender torso was emphasized, as was the hipline, whence flared the new panelled skirt. Hemlines dropped, often with long and short panels or scallops to break this otherwise abrupt change in line. A parallel development was a 'new note in wedding gowns . . . a train that grows out of the gown itself, beginning at the waist-line and continuing a down-at-the-back line.' This usually replaced the court train. With long dresses returned long sleeves, full or fitted.

Long veils, too, were fashionable, to match the dress length, falling from decorative and very individual headdresses. From 1923 to 1927 the diadem headdress in pearls, brilliants or lace, and the turban – now acceptably formal – had been two popular shapes. The resulting neat, cloche-like head shape was framed in a cloud of tulle: lace was now considered old-fashioned by the young bride. Huge bouquets diminished to become more manageable posies of lilies of the valley, orchids, camellias, even nasturtiums and pansies. Garlands or flowers attached to the dress were smart alternatives, and by the mid twenties a simple sheaf of Calla lilies was popular.

Bridesmaids sometimes wore dresses which imitated the style of the bride's, in white, even silver with veils, or pastel colours. Child bridesmaids, very popular in the twenties, more usually wore Second Empire styles, with lacy overdresses and sashes.

Lady Elizabeth Bowes-Lyon's ivory chiffon moiré gown with bands of silver lamé, and Nottingham lace veil over its waist and shoulder trains. B V 1923 *Handley-Seymour*

New emphasis on cut: panelling and all-in-one skirt and train. B V 1926 Douglas Pollard. *Vionnet*

1930

BV 1923 Locher

On previous page:
The slim torso,
short sleeves and
bouffant skirts of
the early twenties.
The bride wears
silver-quilted satin
with trimming
and train in rose-
point lace. Chief
bridesmaid wears
boat-necked,
beribboned blue
moiré, the others
pink taffeta; all
carry garlands.

Ethereal bride, *left*,
in a froth of tulle
edged with satin
ribbon, worn over
a fitted satin
underdress. The
ensemble is
Victorian in
influence, but the
orange blossom
circlet revealing
the bob, and the
billowing net veil,
are entirely 1920.

A V 1920 De
Meyer. *Frances*

AV 1920 De Meyer

FV 1927 Dorys

BV 1927
The chameleon headdress: a merest suggestion, *above left*, in satin ribbon; *below left*, the turban, now considered formal enough for a wedding; *centre*, the diadem which was one of the most popular shapes of the decade; *above right*, the neat head shape of the late twenties; and *below right*, a family lace veil simply shown to its best advantage.

AV 1924 Steichen

BV 1920 De Meyer

BV 1922 Harriet Meserole. *Paul Poiret*
BV 1928 Claire Avery
FV 1926 A. E. Marty. *Jean Magnin*

Opposite, Poiret's design in silver cloth and
brocade for his niece's wedding, with eastern
turban and dropped shoulder line, western
low waist and fashionable long pearls. *This
page*, wedding dresses at their shortest and
simplest: in satin, with embroidery and
ermine-trimmed train, *above right*; in silver
lamé and lace, *below right*, both with the
long sleeves still obligatory in France at this
time. Scalloped hem and down-at-the-back
line, *above*, as the hemline gradually descends
once more.

FV 1926 A. E. Marty

AV 1920 Charlotte Fairchild

'The fates could hardly help smiling on the bride's path when it is flower-strewn by such charming attendant Loves as these', *above*, in dresses of silk faille with écru net and skunk fur trim. Tiny bridesmaids were very fashionable now, such as those *left*, in their Second-Empire-style lace dresses with satin sashes, tucked sleeves and their all-enveloping hats. The bride wears an antique lace veil and has a garland of flowers attached to her dress, a fashionable alternative to a bouquet. The appeal of the *moyen âge* look is demonstrated, *opposite above and below left*, in satin, with nun-like headdresses, even a pectoral cross. A more liberal interpretation, *opposite right*, in cloth of silver with a crystal-embroidered front panel and net cap. The court train has now become very slender by comparison with that of 1920 (*this page left*) and will soon disappear as the skirt acquires an all-in-one train.

FV 1926 *Worth*

BV 1927   BV 1927 *Lanvin*

25

AV 1927 Benito

Two stunning
images by Benito
for the bridal issue
of *Vogue* which
appeared each
spring. *Opposite*,
the Russian-style
headdress, here
with orange
blossom, was a
popular shape. By
the late twenties
the full-length,
slender gown with
long sleeves had
re-emerged, *this
page*, here
trimmed with fur.

AV 1928 Benito

1930

'The bride appears at her loveliest in the new fitted and moulded gowns with long, sweeping lines', noted *Vogue* in 1930. The look was still very neat-headed, with long swathes of tulle or fine lace silhouetting an intricately cut yet simple dress. The tightness of the hipline gradually extended up to the waist and down almost to the knees, which gave a rather fishtail look to the full skirts which flared out below. From 1930 onwards more and more emphasis was given to the upper torso. At first, tight sleeves in fine fabrics might have satin cap sleeves over them; in 1931 they were fuller-topped or leg-o'-mutton, and by 1934 were larger still, long or just below elbow-length. The bodice was emphasized, too, with draped necklines, cape collars, lacy bows, overlay or gathering.

Colour was a fashionable preoccupation: 'colours of greatest chic', noted *Vogue* in 1931, 'are ivory, cream, a flushed pinkish white, palest blue-white and dead-white.' Materials were either satins and silvery lace, or, now more usually, the dull-finish crepe de chine, organdie, lace and chiffon types.

Hairstyles were slightly longer: curls, now reaching the upper neck, peeped from beneath Juliet caps of tulle, lace or beadwork. The veil was long, sometimes even layered, falling from the lower edges of the cap. In 1931 *Vogue* advised readers to avoid 'all complicated and period styles'. However, the nun-like and *moyen âge* looks were important throughout the decade, and by 1938 restraint had been wholly abandoned. *Vogue* advised too, for less formal weddings, that 'when the bride decides to be married in ordinary dress, her best choice is a suit', advice which was to be still more important in wartime.

The influence of the film world was felt in wedding dress design by 1935: 'glamour' became the key word, and the desired effect was dramatic and overstated. Skirts, falling from a tiny waist emphasized still further by narrow, fitted bodices, were puffed out over bouffant underskirts. Shoulder breadth was bold, enlarged by ruffled or tight high necks, leg-o'-mutton or puffed sleeves.

The nun-like look had also acquired a Hollywood gloss: the gown was longer-than-floor-length to give height, elegantly girdled, with a high neckline and long, full sleeves, in the very unecclesiastical satin or jersey. The veil was modelled on the traditional cloak of the Virgin Mary.

Coiffures, too, were undergoing a dramatic change. A high browline, with hair drawn back to leave the brow completely clear, characterized the decade. Hair was rolled back to frame the face and form a foundation for a diadem, a few flowers, or a headdress made from stiffened tulle. Alternatively, curls were piled on top of the head, and ornamented with clusters of cellophane, silk or fresh flowers. The veil was fastened to the back or top of the headdress, often with a section which could cover the face.

By the time that the film version of 'Gone with the Wind' was released in

The ultimate in Hollywood glamour: pearly slipper satin, swathed and folded into a dramatic bustle which is scattered with a trail of vivid roses. Clusters of roses adorn the veil. B V 1939 Rawlings. *Motley*

1939, Victoriana had swept into bridal fashion with a rustle of petticoats. Waists were nipped in still further, petticoats were worn over crinolines and some designs even had additional panniers and bustles. Femininity in its most exaggerated form was the essential, with emphasis on a very stylized, voluptuous figure – bosomy and hippy – which was pure nostalgia. *Vogue* suggested further devices: 'leg-o'-mutton sleeves – they make your throat look delicate. Dog-collars of pearls, to reach almost up to your ears. Guipure lace, dripping with romance. Petticoats edging shyly into sight with each foot-fall down the aisle. Long opera gloves.'

Parchment and off-white were still bridal choices, but purest white underwent a revival in the closing years of the decade. Fabrics were varied and luxurious: heavy laces, molten gold blistered lamé, marquisette, velvet, jersey, bengaline, taffeta, organza. Bouquets changed style, too. *Vogue* sounded the death-knell of the giant bouquet in 1932: 'the shower bouquet, unless magnificently done, is apt to be a messy bunch of flowers'. Casual sheaves of gladioli, lilies, white roses, stocks, narcissi, violets and azaleas took over. Victorian posies of real, silk or shiny cellophane flowers were the most popular by 1939.

'Picturesque attendants' frocks have given way to the smart, wearable evening frock that will finish life as such', said *Vogue* in 1931. Bridesmaids were usually adults now, and *Vogue* emphasized the wear-again aspect of their gowns: the trains could later be shortened or removed, and on the big day the dress was worn with a demure bolero. Mid-decade, calf-length bridesmaids' dresses were temporarily in favour. Colours and fabrics were daring: pink chiffon with bands of black lace, white satin embroidered with blue and green, bold prints, bordeaux and midnight-blue satins, and ostrich feather trim. In 1938 *Vogue* recommended the bride to have 'bridesmaids in velveteen dirndls – very Old World – in all shades of violet.' Like the bride's dress, these had very tight bodices and neat waists.

A new problem for the bride in the thirties resulted from the popularity of make-up. Worn in the twenties, too, it had now become essential rather than just fun or daring. *Vogue* was full of advice on how to make up for the day, who was the best helper to employ, which colours to use, how much to wear. But there remained, as *Vogue* noted in 1935 'one frightful snag . . . where to put handkerchief, mirror and compact. . . . At that hour in your life when you want to look most beautiful you must stand alone without a single beauty aid, without even a little pocket mirror. Some brides take a tiny flat compact and hold it with their bouquets, handing both over to the bridesmaid when the time comes. Better, really, just to forget it for the short half hour of the ceremony, and get a bridesmaid or someone to bring your handbag into the vestry for a final glance of reassurance before you face the wedding march.'

Startling pink chiffon and black lace bridesmaid's dress. BV 1937 Cecil Beaton. *Heim*

A satin cap and silver-sequinned veil frame a bouquet of gold-tipped wax lilies. BV 1935 Cecil Beaton. *Norman Hartnell*

1940

BV 1931

Regal silhouette on long, lean lines, *above*, in satin and fine lace. The instep length, geometric panelling, all-in-one train and the neat head shape created by the juliet cap were all high fashion.

The bridesmaid wears a low-backed gown with more detailed panelling than the bride's, which was designed to be an evening dress later, with a bolero for the ceremony.

BV 1935

BV 1930

A gown of 'sculptured loveliness', *right and far right*, in satin with lace vestee. The front view shows how the waist was now being emphasized, the back view how the tight hipline was extending downwards, too. Long sleeves were very smart in 1930. The broad-shouldered look was important by 1935, *above*, emphasis here given by a wide cape collar with high neck. The waist is cinched, and unpressed pleats give a smooth hip silhouette. The gown now reaches the floor, not the upper instep, and the neat head shape has disappeared in favour of a heap of curls piled on top of the head, and a headdress worn well back.

31

BV 1935 Cecil Beaton. *Joe Strassner/Contessa*

Mrs Robert Laycock, *opposite*, among the billows of her lace-overlaid wedding dress with cinched waist, vast skirt, fitted bodice and stiff pearl yoke. Her leg-o'-mutton sleeves are stiffened and full, her headdress of flowers worn well back. Madame Jean Ternynck, *this page*, in a glamorous theatrical pose, wearing a fluid stream of satin, with shawl collar.

FV 1934 Georges Saad. *Jodelle*

Bride and bridesmaids all in white, *overleaf*, she in satin with shells and cellophane flowers caught in her veil, which is fastened in a pile of flowers and curls on top of her head. Her bridesmaids wear full organza dresses with cinched-in waists to match the bride's, and carry bead bouquets.

BV 1937 Eric. *Schiaparelli (bride), Paquin (bridesmaids)*

BV 1938 Rawlings. *Worth*

Gold-plated bride, *left,* in molten gold blistered lamé with huge sleeves, sinuous skirt and silk arum lilies at the neck. More lilies form a diadem high above the brow, holding a vast, fine net train. *Opposite left,* Blanche-of-Castile-style robe, longer than long, with satin cloak/veil to match, falling from a jewelled crown. More star-struck wedding design *opposite centre*: high neckline and pearls, full sleeves, a cellophane bouquet and 'Greek' stiffened tulle headdress; *opposite right,* vampish nun-like wedding outfit with Madonna-style cloak which is in fact an extension of the skirt.

BV 1938 Rawlings. *Worth*

Gold-plated bride, *left*, in molten gold blistered lamé with huge sleeves, sinuous skirt and silk arum lilies at the neck. More lilies form a diadem high above the brow, holding a vast, fine net train. *Opposite left*, Blanche-of-Castile-style robe, longer than long, with satin cloak/veil to match, falling from a jewelled crown. More star-struck wedding design *opposite centre*: high neckline and pearls, full sleeves, a cellophane bouquet and 'Greek' stiffened tulle headdress; *opposite right*, vampish nun-like wedding outfit with Madonna-style cloak which is in fact an extension of the skirt.

FV 1939 André Durst. *Lanvin*   BV 1936 Horst. *Eno*   BV 1936 André Durst. *Vionnet*

FV 1939 André Durst. *Lelong*

FV 1939 André Durst. *Heim*

The Scarlett O'Hara look had swept into wedding fashion by summer 1939: an exaggerated, feminine silhouette, achieved with exactly the same stiffening, padding and cinching devices which were to be called the 'New Look' in 1947. The button-front bodice, *opposite*, has panniers attached, the sleeves are long and fitted, worn with gloves, and the satin skirt and train are puffed out with layers of petticoats. Hairstyles, in keeping with

FV 1939 André Durst. *Balenciaga*

the Victorian look, are higher, and intricately rolled and curled. The bride carries a neat posy of fabric flowers and net. *Above left*, tulle and rayon moiré crinoline, with a short tunic and gathered shoulderline; *above right*, silk mousseline dress with belted waist, skirt and train with scalloped-edge pleats. The tulle aureole is stiffened to frame the face. The double-ended veil gave a wider frame for the new, very expansive ensemble.

1940

'One marine coming in on ten-day leave stop be patriotic'. Wedding dates were set at the drop of a telegram, dresses shopped for while the champagne cooled (although *Vogue* was bemoaning the dwindling stocks of the latter by 1941). It all made for romance, indeed it was a necessary escape mechanism from the hardships and worries and losses of war. This was a mood which characterized every aspect of weddings during the decade, and the urgency of life made impulsive weddings commonplace. In 1943 *Vogue* published a 'Love Quiz' to help readers differentiate between infatuation and love, 'are you using less lipstick?' and 'do you manage to bring his name and opinions into irrelevant conversations?' being considered crucial questions in making the decision.

During the early years of the war, weddings in America were naturally very different from those in Europe. Although lack of wedding preparation time was a problem there, too, most American brides still had lavish new gowns and veils, as fabric restrictions did not appear until late in the war. In Britain and France the wedding outfit was often an old favourite suit, due to lack of fabric and time, and to coupon restrictions. *Vogue* was full of advice on how to cope with all these problems.

Nineteenth-century styles continued to influence American wedding-dress design. Fitted bodices and full skirts remained. New, though, was the use of finely gathered or draped jersey, which gave fullness, but not the bulk which had characterized the closing years of the thirties. Even taffeta dresses were less bouffant and bolstered, necklines high and simple at first, but later wider, off-the-shoulder. The pompadour hairstyle, a shining roll of hair around the face and nape of the neck, reached shoulder level during the decade. It was a bridal focal point, completed with a diadem, crown or floral arrangement, and short, full veil. Fussy details characterized this period, and *Vogue* gave ideas: 'a helmet of gold thread, or a wreath of gold kid leaves. Or have a showering veil of gold mesh. Ransack Chinese shops for white jade butterflies, or flower-topped hairpins.' Fabrics were jersey, organdie, crepe, brocade, satin, batiste, lawn and lace, in ivory, palest blue, pink, beige, green, mauve and white. Despite hasty weddings (enterprising firms made up dresses in thirty-six hours) and the shadow of war, American *Vogue* was adamant that 'Say what you like, . . . there are few things on earth more satisfactory than a bang-up wedding with The Works. Red carpets and paper rose-leaves. "Lohengrin" and family lace, dry champagne and striped marquees, and a four-piece string orchestra playing waltzes.'

In Britain wedding dresses were not readily obtainable. Furnishing fabrics and lace, unrestricted by coupons, were popular wedding choices. Many brides opted, in any case, for a new suit or coat and hat which would continue to be a useful mufti outfit. For the more traditional bride, *Vogue*

Two very different wartime brides; the bride, *top*, wears traditional white satin and carries a bouquet of lilies. The frugal bride, *above*, is wearing her favourite dress to the wedding and is seen here inspecting her practical, wartime presents. B V 1942

gave this practical advice: 'you can no longer have wedding bells, but if you've set your heart on being married in white, it is still not outside the bounds of possibility. Choose lace – antique or new. What could be lovelier? – and your coupon card will still be intact. The only other way to a white wedding is to wear your mother's or grandmother's dress.' Styles were imitative of those in the many pictures which British *Vogue* lifted from American *Vogue* (French *Vogue* was not published during wartime), and the emphasis was on adapting these designs or existing garments, and on making one's own accessories.

The war over, bridal fashion resumed its importance internationally. The look was based more on romance than sophistication: it was demure and youthful. Perhaps as a result of wartime diet, a much slimmer figure was in fashion. There was, also, a return to the crinoline underskirt, and the waistline, which had begun to extend into a V at the front, sometimes formed a basque. In 1946 and 1947 the line was uncertain, but by the end of the decade a neat shape, simple in design, had been established. The neckline was lower: particularly popular were the sweetheart neckline, draped fichu collar and wide, almost off-the-shoulder shapes. The skirt was bell-shaped, in finer lawns, dotted swiss, poplin and organdie, the bodice simple, a style easily adaptable into a summer evening dress. The Queen's wedding dress, in 1947, was more a ceremonial than a fashion gown. *Vogue* described it as a 'bridal dress in the great tradition: ivory satin starred, with Botticelli-like delicacy and richness, with pearl and crystal roses, wheat, orange blossom.' It was, as a result, very stiff, and had long sleeves slit at the wrist, coming down over the hand. There was a long, square, court train, and a double tulle veil which fell from a diamond tiara.

Bridesmaids had not been much in evidence in wartime, but, mid-decade, grown-up bridesmaids became usual once more. Their dresses tended to match the bride's in mood rather than style. *Vogue* suggested 'mane-length' snoods with bows, ballet slippers, organdie bonnets and long, embroidered gloves for bridesmaids. One smart retinue was dressed in deep brown jersey, swathed Greek-style, while the bride wore a dress with draped bodice, but in stiffer fabric, with a bell-shaped skirt.

Bouquets were not considered important in the forties. In wartime, flowers were not easily obtainable since all available farming land had been put to food production. As an alternative, and also for the hair, fabric flowers were often used, being unrationed. After the war small posies of scented flowers such as lilies of the valley and gardenias, and the ever-popular orchid, were fashionable, although flowers were still not a vital accessory in 1949. *Vogue* said, 'if you're carrying flowers, have a few sweetheart roses at the centre of your white bouquet, or a few blue forget-me-nots.'

The bride's exquisite Belgian lace dress was as lavish as the wedding reception, held around a swimming pool strewn with water-lilies. A V 1947 Jerome Zerbe. *Carrie Munn, John Frederics*

Isabel Benito, daughter of *Vogue* artist Eduardo Benito, wears pale blue, stiff faille. A V 1948 Rawlings

1950

Pompadour hairstyles, *this page*, with very individual headdresses: *left*, a mist of chenille-dot veiling, and *right*, a Hawaiian lei of white fabric carnations wound round the head, with two extra blooms as earrings. For headgear and bouquets, fabric flowers like these were very popular. A romantic American bride of 1940, *opposite*, in an organdie frock with ribbon-banding and fitted bodice, and an organdie bonnet.

AV 1940 Horst. *Herman Patrick Tappé*

AV 1940 Rawlings

AV 1940 Lee Miller. *Lanvin*

BV 1941 Cecil Beaton. *Bianca Mosca*

Simple satin and jersey dresses, *above left and below left* respectively, with pearls and gold bead details: fussy individual touches were a trademark of contemporary design. Headdresses, too, were ornate, veils short, that *left* in fine wool, an idea which British *Vogue* suggested readers could adapt for themselves. Unrationed lace and grey ribbon, *above*, made a traditional wedding dress for Mrs James Gladstone, worn with an antique lace veil simply fastened to the hair. Unusually for wartime, she carried a posy of fresh flowers. Unrestricted glamour, *opposite*, on the other side of the Atlantic, in this boat-neck dress made from lace and thirty-five yards of silk tulle. A single lily and a chou of tulle make an informal headdress.

AV 1941

AV 1940 Horst. *Mabel McIlbain Downs*

The Greek influence, *opposite*. Draped gathers are now sinuous rather than bouffant: Barbara Cushing wears white silk jersey with ruched sleeves, torso and bodice, and a crown of gold and paste sapphires with finest veil. By the end of the forties wedding dresses were simple, youthful, often very demure. The dress, *right*, is made from handkerchief linen with fine lace circling the bell skirt and maidenly bodice. Short sleeves and Peter Pan collar complete the look, so neat that it would easily convert into an evening frock.

AV 1948 *Clare Potter*

BV 1947 Coffin. *Norman Hartnell*

AV 1948 Rawlings. *Cecil Chapman*

The return of emphatically feminine styling after the war, nipped-in curves, draping and long trains again. *Left*, bridesmaids return to the scene, their brown jersey dresses matching the bride's stiffer satin in mood, their draperies echoing those of her bodice. Necklines are beginning to deepen: the portrait neckline of 1948, *above right*, is boldly décolleté, the redingote of satin worn over a lace underdress. *Below right*, a nostalgic, tiered dress with sprays of orange blossom and coiffed veiling.

BV 1947 Coffin. *Bianca Mosca*

H.R.H. Princess Elizabeth's wedding,
1947. *Right*, her dress in embroidered
satin with a sweetheart neckline, and
far right, a bridesmaid's dress,
influenced by Winterhalter's
paintings, in ivory silk tulle with
fichu neckline.

BV 1947 John Ward. *Norman Hartnell*

BV 1947 *Norman Hartnell*

The Princess and Lieutenant Philip Mountbatten leave the
Abbey, *above*, the Princess's diadem tiara holding a tiered tulle
veil. Her shoe was drawn for *Vogue* as a symbol of good luck.
Vogue said: 'we hope that their lives will be as smooth as its
satin – their spirit as bright as its buckle – and their happiness as
perfect as its shape.'

BV 1947 John Ward. *Rayne*

1950

A thrush-egg blue, short bridesmaid's dress worn with a pompon posy and chignon cap. BV 1954 John Sadovy. *Julian Rose*

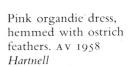

Pink organdie dress, hemmed with ostrich feathers. AV 1958 *Hartnell*

The sought-after bridal appearance of the fifties was, according to *Vogue*, a 'fragile delicacy and a deliciously gentle femininity', achieved not only by exquisite ensembles, but by long hours in beauty salons, particularly a 'Day of Beauty' just prior to the great event. In fact, the resulting look now seems far from 'gently' feminine, but sophisticated and poised. Now that 'off-the-peg' wedding dresses were so usual, *Vogue* played an increasingly important role in guiding eager brides-to-be towards the shops which would be most useful to them, as well as in giving its traditional guidance on fashionable styles, fabrics and accessories.

'The way to look at a wedding, when you're the bride, is as beautiful as your husband knows you are, as beautiful as you've always dreamed of being. The dress to crystallize that beauty, as timelessly right as in a Renaissance portrait, need not be expensive, or worn only once.' Nylon, the wedding discovery of the decade, was inexpensive by comparison with silk, and perhaps explains why lavish layering remained fashionable for so long, and why 'white-white', attainable only in synthetics, and which *Vogue* described as 'dazzling, as fresh as a newly scrubbed choirboy', was the smartest bridal colour.

The fashionable wedding silhouette changed subtly rather than dramatically during the fifties. In 1950 the dress could be long, or mid-calf-length, with a billowing skirt and fitted bodice cut to show both waist- and bustline to maximum advantage. Variation lay in the rounded, portrait, caped or sweetheart neckline and in the full, dolman, long or short tight sleeves. There was a strong move towards sleevelessness, accompanied by elbow-length gloves. Décolleté evening dresses were rendered bridal with the addition of bertha jackets, lace blouses or spencers. Such adaptability was an important consideration throughout the fifties, and wedding fashion thus followed the evening mode closely. Special underwear was vital to achieve the necessary silhouette: a strapless waist-pincher gave a clean line to the hip, and a crinoline was essential. 'All stores ask that the crinoline be bought before the dress and be worn at every fitting', noted *Vogue* in 1951. Petticoats were ornamented with ribbons and embroidery so that they could show themselves with impunity when the bride picked up her train to dance. Trains were worn most often for dramatic effect at large weddings, in fabrics such as stiff nylon tulle and organdie, rayon satin, guipure and fine rose-point laces, broderie anglaise, organza shantung.

'The long trailing veil has almost disappeared', said *Vogue* in 1951. 'The exceptions, of course, the great heirloom laces. Most veils are finger-tip length; some ankle-length'. Short veils tended to be very full, often of tulle, although lace was still popular. The veil could be attached to the coiffure, or fastened to a simple headdress: real or fabric flowers, a plain circlet or a circle of old lace. Hairstyles were higher and fuller, long hair drawn back into a soft chignon, or cut in a fringe, with looped-back sides. Shoes were now very much on show, and matched the wedding dress in their angular pointed toes and high slender heels. They were made in dyed satin, or in fabric to match the dress.

'Headdresses are always perched high on the crown of the head, perfect beginnings to the thrust-forward look in dresses loved everywhere, the backward weight of them balancing a beautifully poised head', noted *Vogue* in 1956, as back emphasis and trains became increasingly important. The front of the skirt became flatter, with side pleats to widen the hip line. The waistline moved upwards, often becoming an empire line with a flat bow emphasizing its new position. The hem of the skirt was lifted slightly at the front, increasing the effect of the cascade of skirt and train at the back. As an alternative to the ubiquitous strapless, sleeveless, very bare bodices of many wedding gowns came the stand-up collar, dipping to a buttoned V at the front. A simpler, starkly dramatic look was appearing, too, sculptured from heavy satin or brocade, with long shoulder train, neat headdress in the shape of a pillbox, a flat bow or a tiara – the latter now becoming established as grandest wedding headgear.

Hairstyles grew higher still, with flowers fastened in the chignon and veil attached at both sides of the head, or knotted to form a headdress as well. Veils themselves were pastel-coloured, dotted, spattered with flower-heads or brushed with petals. Bouquets began the decade as sizeable bunches, imitating the old shower bouquet. Gradually their breadth decreased, and their length increased. The fan-shaped bouquet was popular in 1956, but later simple arrangements such as bunches of blowsy roses, posies of lilies of the valley, took over.

Short bridesmaids' dresses, less formal, but similar to the bride's in cut, were *de rigueur* at first, lengthening gradually over the decade. They were full and stiff, crinolined, in taffetas and nets, worn with simple, flowered headdresses. Numerous attendants were fashionable: married or single, large or small. Lady Rosemary Spencer-Churchill, who married in 1953, had seven little bridesmaids dressed in white, empire-line organdie frocks, and five pages in white satin suits. Warp-printed silk taffeta, embroidered organdie, and broderie anglaise were some of the most popular fabric choices for bridal retinues. *Vogue*'s recommendation was for 'a bouquet of bridesmaids, dressed with all the tint and prettiness of a garden wedding, each in a different colour over layers of white net: palest peach, yellow, powder blue, mauve, pink and aquamarine.'

For a civil ceremony, a banana yellow wool and silk dress and crescent headdress. BV 1955 Hammarskiöld. *Dior*

Starkly simple cut and family jewels. FV 1958 *Mellerio*

1960

AV 1951 Norman Parkinson. *Celeste*

Baby bridesmaid's dress, *opposite*, in creamy Swiss organdie embroidered with blue ferns and edged with lace. Like the bride's dress, it has a bouffant skirt; the ruffled neck, puffed sleeves and high waistline had by now become established as 'traditional' wear for young bridesmaids. Traditional now, too, were the velvet Little Lord Fauntleroy suit for pageboys, *right*, here with organdie collar and cuffs and fringed cummerbund, and the Kate Greenaway suit, *below*, worn with buckled, patent shoes. The wedding dress, *below*, has the up-at-the-front and down-at-the-back look characteristic of the late fifties.

BV 1958 Norman Parkinson. *Patricia Anne (page), Margot Bywaters (bride)*

FV 1955 Sabine Weiss. *Christian Dior*

AV 1953 Doisneau.
Schiaparelli

The 'bouffancy of a
beautiful new kind,
almost unbelievably
wide, and borne on
crinolines'. *Left*, the
Viscountess d'Harcourt
in a short dress of satin
and tulle with the
fashionable tight sleeves
and Normandy head-
dress. More satin,
with old family lace,
opposite, made Edna
Haldeman Leib's
wedding dress. The
fitted bodice, skirt full
all round and simple
fastening of the veil to
the coiffure were all
fashion notes of 1951.

AV 1951 Joffé.
Elizabeth Arden

FV 1959 Jacques Verroust.
Rébé

Young, fringed haircut, *opposite*, as opposed to the more sophisticated drawn-back style, *right*; there was a new movement now to produce special styles for the teens and early twenties age group, who wanted their own look. Wedding designs naturally formed part of this movement. The informal cluster of roses, gypsophila, lilies of the valley and lilac, *opposite*, was modelled on the traditional Ukranian bridal headress. The lace and flower veil and satin gown, *right*, were inspired by Velásquez' paintings. The rounded neckline, fitted bodice and long gloves were also important fashion notes.

FV 1956 Sabine Weiss.
Lanvin-Castillo

AV 1950 Penn. *Mrs Sollier*

AV 1957 Penn. *Sophie*

'At my wedding I'd like my dress to be traditional . . . but I'd like to look fresh and of-this-year, too, not like a period piece', was the perennial bridal wish of the fifties, as reiterated by *Vogue*. It was one which was generally fulfilled, too, as the dresses *on this page and opposite* show. *Far left*, Mrs Sohier in an off-the-shoulder décolletage sheltered for the service by a crescent of cape, but becoming a stunning evening gown later. Over-elbow gloves add further formality, and her veil is elbow-length too. Mrs Cleve Gray, daughter of Mrs Alexander Liberman, *left*, wears a sculptured, finely tucked gown with a coif of tulle falling from an inverted crown of seed pearls. Her bouquet is the fashionably informal cluster of lilies of the valley. *Far left below* portrait-necked satin dress: the sleeves were

BV 1952 Norman Parkinson. *Mercia*

FV 1953 Henry Clarke. *Jean Dessès*

BV 1954 John Sadovy. *Roecliffe & Chapman*

removable to make a halter-necked
ball gown. 'Lucky' dress, *opposite
below centre*, embroidered all over
with four-leaved clovers, has the
flatter skirt front, fuller back, which
became popular. The tiara, too, was
to be the standard wedding
headdress. Heavy guipure lace,
opposite below right, worn with a mass
of veiling. *Below* is a 'wedding dress
in a long line of tradition – the skirt
full and full-length, in white
organdie with a woven stripe of
denser organdie.' Very
contemporary, however, is the
evening-dress effect of the satin
underdress, modestly covered with
the high-necked organdie bodice for
the big day. The new line by the late
fifties, *right*: up at the front to show
off neat ankles in arched shoes, down
at the back in a long sweep, simply
sculptured in brocaded gold lamé.

AV 1952 Prigent. *Jay Thorpe*

FV 1958 Donald Silverstein. *Laroche*

1960

White satin dress and water-lily headdress. A V 1960 Penn

Pinky beige lace dress topped with a headdress of pink satin loops and lilies of the valley. F V 1961 Guy Bourdin. *Serge Matta*

'This year's weddings are distinguished by new clear-cut simplicity . . . uncluttered outlines (no frills) stiff veils (short enough to spring up with bouffancy above a sleek hair style), crisp materials (rippling fabrics don't take firm shapes in the same way)', said *Vogue* in 1961. The statuesque, flowing lines of the late fifties were honed down, and were to be refined still further. The 'wear-again' potential of wedding dresses ceased to be a criterion of choice in terms of practicality or fashionability, as more informal evenings became the rule. Long, grand, décolleté evening gowns were out for the young: short, even minidresses, less fuss and finery were in. The wedding dress became very much a one-day, ceremonial institution. As such, in the climate of change and rebellion, the formal white (or almost white) wedding dress could well have disappeared from fashion completely had it not been for the continuing inspiration from couturiers like Balenciaga, and, later, the burst of nostalgia which brought with it a harking back to old customs and styles.

The silhouette which had been popular at the end of the fifties continued on into the early sixties with gradual, subtle modifications. Side-view, it formed a right-angled triangle, with the train and veil forming the hypotenuse. The train could be either a court train, from the shoulder, or merely an extension of the skirt. A looser waistline, either high or in its natural position, became usual. Fullness was of an increasingly stiff and padded type: the skirt front was quite flat, breadth given to the remainder with unpressed pleats or large gathers in interlined fabric. Most popular choices for this were taffeta, rayon or silk satin, organza, dotted swiss, broderie anglaise, linen and cottons. The bodice was still fitted, with what *Vogue* described as a 'gently scooped' neckline – demurely low – cut widely over the shoulders so that sleeves and bodice had the appearance of being cut in one. By 1962 the neckline had begun to acquire a rolled collar. Sleeves were fitted and could be either short or long, the latter often reaching over the top of the hand, ending in a point. Veils were by no means the rule now: cotton, lacy, or even frilled headscarves, broad straw hats, neat flower-covered bonnets or beanie hats covered in fabric to match the dress could replace veiling. The veil, when it appeared, was short and full. Hairstyles were varied: backcombed chignons and buns, long bobs with fringes, hugely frizzed pre-Raphaelite manes, and boyish crops.

The early sixties saw three grand royal weddings. Princess Margaret married in 1960, her Norman Hartnell dress following the current bouffant yet stiff trend, with a fitted bodice, V-neck and long, tight sleeves. Her hair was arranged in a huge, high bun, encircled by the Poltimore tiara. Katherine Worsley's dress, designed by John Cavanagh for her marriage to the Duke of Kent in 1961, had the fashionable low, standaway neckline, fitted bodice and pleated skirt. She and Princess Alexandra, whose dress was also designed by Cavanagh for her wedding in 1963, wore tiaras, now standard royal wedding headgear. Princess Alexandra's dress fabric was woven to include motifs from the lace veil worn in 1919 by Lady Patricia Ramsay, a veil which had been presented to the Princess, but was now too outmoded to wear.

'Wedding dresses have less and less fuss to distract attention from the bride's face: they are gentler, dreamier and simpler than before', wrote *Vogue* in 1964. At times the dress was positively monkish, not quite a seamless garment, but certainly minimally seamed. The waistline was often unmarked, the straight or bell-shaped sleeves were cut in one with the dress, or joined with a straight seam, kaftan-style, and the fabric was plain. By 1966, however, a more romantic, nostalgic mood was beginning to be felt in wedding design. Lace crept back into veiling, headdresses, and eventually into the dress itself. Flowery lace was the most popular choice: the flower motif, symbol of the decade, was appliquéd onto chiffon, or embroidered. 'Little-girl' dresses formed part of this nostalgic mode, very youthful pintucked or buttoned bodices with Peter Pan collars and long, cuffed sleeves. Frills began to reappear on hems and cuffs. Cummerbunds, puffed sleeves and fine cotton lawn all became trademarks of a romanticism which was to last well into the seventies. Hairstyles in this vein were varied. Ringlets were piled up to form a soft chignon with several left to frame the face, or long hair was left loose under a flowered headdress and veil. Fur was a fashionable choice for winter weddings: ermine or white fox with white velvet for the bride, darker furs and velvets for the retinue.

Sixties wedding clothes were by no means entirely conventional. Yves Saint Laurent designed a flower-studded bikini and matching circlet in 1967, to be worn with nothing else but a bouquet and sandals. See-through fabrics were used, too, over minimal underthings. As church weddings were by nature both traditional and formal, they now lost popularity. For civil ceremonies, it was quite common for the bride and groom to wear jeans; other choices for the bride were loose Indian clothes or 'antique' dresses (which usually dated from the twenties).

Bridesmaids were still usual at more formal weddings, and tended to be young. They wore pared-down versions of the bride's outfit, with no train. The Hon. Lucinda Lambton's bridesmaids in 1965 wore moss-green velvet with furred muffs and hats for her winter wedding, while she wore white velvet and ermine. One set of bridesmaids in 1967 wore divided skirts, which were rather daring for a formal wedding. With the return of frills, tucks and ribbons, the look had now left the unblurred silhouette of the early sixties far behind.

Frilly, flounced wedding and bridesmaid's minidresses with little-girl sleeves. BV 1968 Peter Rand. *Deborah Newall*

Grace Coddington marries Michael Chow in leaf-green panné velvet. BV 1969. *The Sweetshop*

1970

FV 1962 Maurice Pascal. *Yves Saint Laurent*

FV 1962 Maurice Pascal. *Pierre Balmain*

The triangular silhouette of the early sixties, *above and left*, then considered very unconventional. The loose waistline, dropping at the back, short straight sleeves, short train and back emphasis in the form of appliquéd lilies, *left*, are all characteristic of the time. The fabric is crimped cotton. Headscarves began bridal life as Yves Saint Laurent trademarks, but were generally adopted later. The version, *above*, was made from white cotton lace and piqué, with a high waistline and a 'Velásquez' bonnet. Catherine Deneuve, *opposite*, models a nylon organza see-through wedding dress with flower appliqué, so loose that it is headdress, dress and veil all in one.

FV 1964 Bert Stern. *Venet*

BV 1962 Carapetian. *Cockayne, Mad Hatter*

The one-day-only wedding dress in the sixties: bubbly brocade, *left*, provides a perfect back-drop for a cascade of flounces fanning from the roll collar. The bridesmaid's collar is trimmed with a single bow in yellow ottoman. Ice-white peau-de-soie, *above*, provides a simpler surface from which to hang the waist train and the two floppy bows which fall on either side. A plaited peau-de-soie pillbox adds texture. The bridesmaid's simulated wild silk dress is in vivid amber, buttoned from neck to hem and teamed with a matching skull cap. Simplest of all is the graceful dress with sweeping train, *opposite*, of heavy wild silk. The train, emphasized by the dress's clean lines, hangs from the neck and is caught at the waist. The bridesmaid's crimson red dress is low backed and has elbow-length sleeves. Hairstyles are neat, swept back into chignons, or up into knots.

BV 1962 Carapetian. *Jean Varon*

BV 1962 Peter Rand. *Muriel Martin*

BV 1963 Vernier. *Muriel Martin*

Elaborate headgear and simply cut wedding dresses drew attention to the bride's face. *Vogue* recommended that the 'newest way for brides to look is *natural*. Skins that are subject through excitement to pallor or high colour must not be left to chance. Find a thin foundation that looks like nature improved.' The wide-brimmed hat, *left*, flattered the face, drew attention from the simple nylon organza frock and Victorian posy. Two more alternatives to the veil, *opposite: above*, a tiny white bathing-cap frosted with thick ribbon on net, with a bunch of lilies of the valley and a trail of satin ribbon on one side, *below*, development of Saint Laurent's kerchief, here thick with frills of broderie anglaise, tying under the chin in a 'Puritan' satin bow. *Far right*, extraordinary tulle headdress and veil crown the tight-bodiced, panniered satin dress by Cardin.

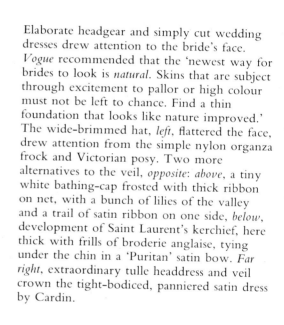

BV 1964 Donald Silverstein. *Dolores*

BV 1964 Donald Silverstein. *Reed Crawford*
FV 1960 Henry Clarke. *Cardin*

BV 1969 David Thorpe. *Young's Dress Hire*
BV 1966 Barry Weller. *Deborah Newall*
BV 1968 Peter Rand. *Ellis*

A note of fantasy is added to the spring bride's dress *opposite left*, by the addition of garlands of flowers around the hem and sleeves. For the less flamboyant bride, *opposite right*, clouds of delicate lace and a flounced hem are equally romantic. Flowers trim the long veil of the warmer dress of white wool, *above*. The dress itself has deep cuffs and a bodice trimmed with pleated frills. Most fragile of all is the chiffon sheath, *right*, which reveals a taffeta slip banded with satin beneath.

BV 1966 Patrick Ward. *Donerica*

B V 1960 Brian Duffy. *Norman Hartnell*

Tiaras became traditional wear for the smartest society weddings. Princess Margaret, *above*, wore the Poltimore tiara, specially acquired for her wedding, around a high bun, holding a mass of satin-edged tulle veiling. The Hon. Lucinda Lambton's tiara, *opposite*, was edged with ermine, as was her long, medieval, velvet robe, for her winter wedding. The attendants wore green velvet with furred muffs and hats. Lady Rachel Pakenham's tiara, *right*, was a family one. She wore a maxi coat-dress circled with white fox; the bridesmaids' dresses were simply cut, too, tent-shaped with silver brocade. Her ringlets were extremely fashionable.

B V 1968 Norman Parkinson. *M. Berman*

BV 1963 Vernier. *Muriel Martin*

The little girl look and the not so-little-girl look; innocent Peter Pan collar and cuffed sleeves on a broderie anglaise shirtwaist wedding dress, *left*, contrast with the barest bikini bride by Saint Laurent, *opposite*, her accessories a boyish crop, flowers and sandals. *Opposite right*, another demure look for this bride. She wears a slub rayon dress with Edwardian sleeves of organdie petals and a frothy white beanie.

FV 1967 Bert Stein. *Yves Saint Laurent*

BV 1963 Vernier. *Nettie Vogues*

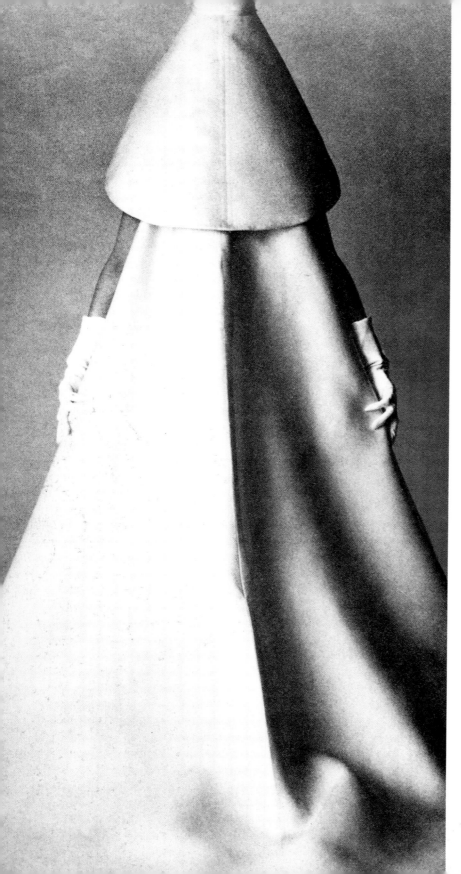

AV 1967 David Bailey. *Balenciaga*

BV 1967 Norman Parkinson. *John Bates/Jean Varon*

The wide span of wedding gear in fashion at the end of the sixties, *this page and opposite*. *Opposite*, the simplest, monkish gown with no waistline, untrimmed neck, and bell sleeves, in marble-white crepe. The snood furthers the medieval mood. Inspiration from Balenciaga, *left*, the ultimate in sixties sculptured clothes: ivory gazar carved in a shoulder-circling headdress, a taut long oval train; in front the dress falls straight from tiny sleeves. *Above*, traditionally white but revolutionary wedding look: minidress with camisole top, wrapped in a cloud of finest organza, fastened with a bow on the top of the head.

BV 1966 Patrick Ward.
Sarah Percival

Nostalgia and romance: a new style of bridal fashion photography accompanied the new mood. The demure, scooped neckline, *left and opposite* was not new, but the cummerbund, tucked and buttoned front, softer gathers and frilled hem *left*, the guipure lace and slim shape, *right*, mark the beginning of a sweeter, softer look. Both dresses still show signs of the 'backward pull' shape so popular in the late fifties and early sixties, the former in its veil, the latter its guipure lace train.

BV 1966 Patrick Ward.
Emens

1970

Twenties-influenced design: silk under-trousers and tunic with a lace poncho veil. FV 1978 Didier Destal. *Sonia Rykiel.*

The Princess of Wales' handmade silk slippers with lace rosettes, 542 sequins, 134 pearls, fluted heels. BV 1981 Theo Bergstrom. *Clive Shilton*

The romance begun in the sixties now blossomed, at first restrained and understated, but later culminating in the fragile puff of a dress which Lady Diana Spencer chose for her fairytale marriage to the Prince of Wales in 1981. The institution of marriage was much discussed, questioned and analysed, and apparently not found wanting despite a marked increase in the divorce rate: marriage figures tremored only slightly. Nostalgia was an important note in mainstream fashion during the seventies and early eighties – perhaps as a result of the stultifying effect of economic recession – but nowhere was it more emphasized than in bridal fashion, doubtless a reflection on the current statistical uncertainty of marital bliss after the big day. As tradition and formality came back into fashion, so did religious wedding ceremonies and all the theatre, grandeur, bridesmaids and fuss that surround them. And it all took a great deal of time. Georgiana Boothby devoted 100 days to preparing for her wedding in 1976, which she described as 'a single event with only one performance, no understudies, no retakes.'

At the opening of the decade wedding dresses were soft and filmy. The pared-down, monkish silhouette gradually acquired detail and suppleness. The dress was long and slender, either unwaisted, or with a narrow, gathered skirt loosely pulled in with a soft bow or belt. It consisted of an underdress like a petticoat, leaving the arms and neck bare, and a dress in filmy net, chiffon, lace or embroidered silk or cotton. Sleeves were either long and straight, not tightly fitted, or puffed. By 1974 frills were returning, to sleeve ends, to the neck, even running from waist to shoulder, in soft rather than crisp fabrics so that they fell in soft folds. The overall effect was both dreamy, in the soft translucent fabric draping, and sensual, in the emphasis on the body beneath, which, free of any boning or bolstering with net and crinolines, shaped the dress. Hairstyles were still often the bun or chignon, finished with fresh or fabric flowers, or with a tiara. Veils tended to be long, and hats were a nostalgic alternative, with dotted veiling.

By 1976 skirts were becoming much fuller, and what had begun as a little frill on the hemline had become a deep flounce, even a series of flounces. Sleeves, too, were fuller, gathered at the shoulder and also at the cuff, into a narrow band with yet more frills over the hand. Lawn was a popular fabric, also fine lace and nylon. Hairstyles were much more natural, hair left to hang long and loose, or softly curled with a fresh flower circlet perched atop: Olde-Worlde touches permeated the event itself: ponies and traps were used to transport bride and mock-Edwardian-suited groom to the reception.

All restraint had vanished by 1980. Skirts billowed over layers of petticoats, stiff, shimmery silks with pastel details brightened church aisles, flowers played a role as major as at the outset of the decade. Retro was the overwhelming theme of wedding attire, in blends taken from various epochs. Thirties-style glamour was sported in the form of sequinned bodices and caps, long, elegant gloves and sinuous silk satin gowns. Accent on Victorian and Edwardian styles brought a revival of pure silk for wedding dresses, in all its forms from taffeta to slipper satin. 'Antique' lace and modern silk were used to make mock Edwardian styles, either high-necked and worn with a brooch, or, more usually, low necked. As Victoriana acquired a more important role, the décolleté and shoulder emphasis became still more important, and short, full sleeves gave even more weight.

Lady Diana Spencer's dress in 1981 rode the crest of the wave, bringing the bridal and mainstream fashion mood into sharp focus. Her dress was a blend of old and new: the British designers (David and Elizabeth Emanuel) young, the techniques and skills used both old and traditional. The dress's demurely décolleté fitted bodice was boned, laden with antique lace, sequins, and a double lace and silk ruffle. The skirt was hugely gathered, with layers of fine silk net to hold it out. The court train, in heavy paper taffeta like the dress, was twenty-five feet long. Lady Diana wore a family tiara with her long veil, and her hair was arranged in her everyday, practical bob.

Shoulder emphasis became still more important in 1982 and 1983. Wide, frilled necklines rested on the very edge of the shoulders. When dresses had sleeves – and sleeveless dresses worn with short gloves were popular – they were full, either three-quarter-length, with a frilled hem, or leg-o'-mutton. Volume with crinolines and petticoats was still the rule for skirts, and flat or low-heeled pumps. Pastel silks now began to form the body of the dress, not merely the trimmings, and gold lamé, pearl embroidery, appliquéd lace were all important. Low necklines called for jewellery, and the perennial pearls came into their own again, often in the form of a treble-string choker. Some brides opted for no veil, others for a long, dramatic sweep of silk net.

Flowers played an increasing role in wedding ceremonies during the late seventies and early eighties. The bride's bouquet was in the form of a Victorian posy, a long Edwardian trail of flowers, or a loose bunch, depending on the style of dress. Flowers for the hair were now often scented blooms arranged in circlets, or clusters. Bridesmaids carried neat posies, or miniature baskets laden with flowers and ivies. In the early seventies, print dresses had been a popular choice for bridesmaids in summer, velvet in winter. By the end of that decade, however, styles, fabrics and colours imitated those of the bride's dress.

By 1983 mainstream fashion had begun to take a turn away from nostalgia and to move in a more clean-cut, masculine direction, but wedding dresses remained a fashion in their own right. The bride could choose from historical, retro, glamorous and romantic looks; the huge variety available catered for the fulfilment of even the wildest romantic dreams. As *Vogue* said, 'It can never be too luxurious, a dress for the most beautiful day of your life.'

Chinese-style dress and exotic sequinned headdress. FV 1981 Arthur Elgort. *Scherrer*

Velvet and satin tulip-skirted dress and heart-shaped hairstyle. IV 1982 André Rau. *Claude Montana*

1980...

Queen of the Night, *previous page left*, in stunning aubergine faille dress of early nineteenth-century style, worn with jewelled crown and a mass of veiling. Humorous taffeta and lace dress, *previous page, right*, worn with fashionable punk hairstyle and lace-up boots.

FV 1981 Arthur Elgort. *Yves Saint Laurent*

IV 1983 Neil Kirk. *Sogno*

The soft, supple styles shaped by the body beneath, *right*. The dresses are layered, swathed with fine organdie, dotted net, lace, flocked and embroidered net.

FV 1978 Elliott Erwitt. *Cardin*

BV 1983 Terence Donovan. *Yves Saint Laurent*

Designer wedding dresses in two different moods. Yves Saint Laurent's dress, *opposite*, is a slim, lace sheath overlaid with layers and layers of white tulle with a pink satin bow at the waist. The headdress of white daisies is tinged with silver to match the huge glistening glass heart worn at the neck. More sophisticated in cut, yet youthful with its pantaloon hemline, is the pearl grey taffeta dress with pierette collar and shaped bodice, *this page*. The floating net veil is attached to a cluster of curls with a bow.

IV 1983 Peter Knapp. *Basile*

BV 1971 Christa Peters. *Bellville Sassoon*

Two nostalgic wedding ensembles: *left*, a very Edwardian frock with high, frilled neckline, front tucks, long sleeves gathered into frilled cuffs, and goffered skirt and shoulder cape, in silk paper taffeta. The wide-brimmed hat is laden with ostrich feathers and dotted veiling. Still more retrospective is the Watteau-style gown designed by Karl Lagerfeld, *opposite*, for Patricia Tiné's wedding with François de Courson. Complete with sacque back, the dress's silhouette was a faithful reproduction carried out in cotton satin and Valenciennes lace, but the frilled headscarf added a touch of the present.

FV 1976 Karl Lagerfeld. *Karl Lagerfeld*

pour Patricia
flots de rubans
de valenciennes
bouillonnés
batiste
bracelet fait comme le tour de cou, piqué de fleurs
falache
Paris mars 76
robe en satin de coton piqué
mariage à Vaudreuil
juin 76

IV 1982 Giovanni Gastel.
Raffaella/Davida

Two romantic looks popular
in the early eighties. On *this
page*, stiff silk taffeta in an
Edwardian vein, with
shoulder emphasis in the full,
puffed sleeves gathered into a
fitted long cuff. The bodice
imitates a lingerie blouse in its
fine beading, the bright sash
and pompon shoes add an
eighties touch. Victoriana,
right, shaped this fine cotton
lawn dress with flounced hem,
bodice and sleeves with lace
inserts. New, however, is the
interpretation of a traditional
posy in silvered paper, and
the softly frizzed hairstyle
with informal flowered
circlet.

IV 1982 Barry Lategan.
Raffaelle

BV 1976 Eric Boman. *Pierre Cardin*

FV 1981 Arthur Elgort. *Per Spook*

IV 1982 Steve Hiett. *Ennio Castellani*

The bride in anticipation and action.
Georgiana Russell, *opposite*, serene and
composed before her wedding to Brooke
Boothby in 1976. Her dress has the
fashionable straight sleeves and semi-
transparent upper layer with surface effect in
the embroidery and appliquéd flower petals.
Her court train, fastened with two blue bows,
replaced a veil. Fullness became important for
wedding dresses, movement too, in the frilled
taffeta sleeves, *above*, the huge skirt and tulle-
frilled neckline, *above right*, and the train and
immense veil, *right*. Taffeta was the most
popular choice for summer weddings now,
satin and fur (here white bison, *right*) for
winter.

FV 1979 Horst. *Pierre Balmain*

BV 1981 Patrick Lichfield. *Emanuel*

The dress, *left and right*, source of many months' speculation, seen in all its splendour, and worn by the most romantic bride of all. Its taffeta surface was laden with 10,000 pearls and sequins embroidered by hand, and exquisite antique and specially worked lace, yet floated lightly on layers of knitted silk tulle. Her long veil fell from the Spencer family tiara. The pages wore 1868 Royal Navy Cadet full dress uniforms, indigo and white, and the bridesmaids' dresses were similar to the bride's, with higher necklines, in finer silk. Flowers played a major role: the bride carried an Edwardian-sized bouquet, the bridesmaids posies or baskets of flowers, and wore bright flowers in their hair. Tiniest bridesmaid, *below*, Clementine Hambro.

Overleaf: All dressed up and nowhere to go: dreamy taffeta ribbon frills, velvet, satin and grosgrain.

FV 1981 Arthur Elgort. *Cardin*

BV 1981 Felix Topolski. *Emanuel*